COOL careers
for girls

in Sports

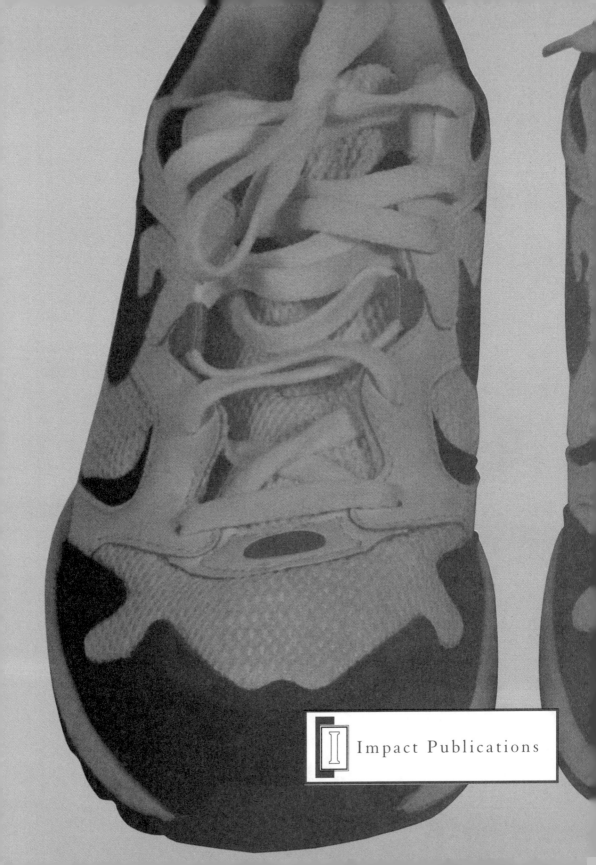

Impact Publications

COOL
careers
for
girls
in
Sports

Ceel Pasternak & Linda Thornburg

Library of Congress Cataloging-in-Publication Data

Pasternak, Ceel, 1932-
     Cool careers for girls in sports / Ceel Pasternak & Linda Thornburg.
        p. cm.
     Includes bibliographical references (p.) and index.
     Summary: Profiles ten women who work in the field of sports, in such
     jobs as ski instructor, athletic director, and referee, and explains
     their duties and how they prepared for and got their positions.
     ISBN 1-57023-107-9 (hardcover)—ISBN 1-57023-104-4 (softcover)
     1. Sports for women—Vocational guidance—Juvenile literature. [1. Sports
     for women—Vocational guidance. 2. Occupations. 3. Vocational guidance]
     I. Thornburg, Linda, 1949- .
     II. Title.
GV709.P25 1998
796'.023'73—DC21   98-48613
                                                      CIP
                                                       AC

Publisher: For information on Impact Publications, including current and forthcoming publications, authors, press kits, bookstore, and submission requirements, visit Impact's Web site: www.impactpublications.com

Publicity/Rights: For information on publicity, author interviews, and subsidiary rights, contact the Public Relations and Marketing Department: Tel. 703/361-7300 or Fax 703/335-9486.

Sales/Distribution: All paperback bookstore sales are handled through Impact's trade distributor: National Book Network, 15200 NBN Way, Blue Ridge Summit, PA 17214, Tel. 1-800-462-6420. All other sales and distribution inquiries should be directed to the publisher: Sales Department, IMPACT PUBLICATIONS, 9104-N Manassas Dr., Manassas Park, VA 20111-5211, Tel. 703/361-7300, Fax 703/335-9486, or E-mail: coolcareers@impactpublications.com

Book design by Guenet Abraham

Dedicated to all the women and
men who helped pave the way for
women athletes

Contents

Until a few years ago, for a girl to want to have a full-time career and make her living in sports was unusual and daring. Today, that's changing. The world of sports is opening up in a wonderful way for women—and it will only get better. The popularity of women's performances in the Olympics and in women's professional basketball, which formed in the United States in 1996, has shown that women's sports can be big business. That's good news for any girl who wants a sports career, because the more money that surrounds women's sports, the more job opportunities there will be for all sorts of women's sport professionals—players, coaches, referees and officials, trainers, sports agents, sports psychologists, and team support staff such as administrators and publicists.

If you're thinking about playing and competing in individual and team sports, you have more professional opportunities these days but it is still difficult to make a living, and it is very competitive. Not long ago, women active in high school and college sports had few choices after graduation, even if they competed in the Olympics. Going professional was mostly limited to individual sports like golf, tennis, skating, and skiing—tough careers even today to break into. Some women athletes, in team sports such as basketball and soccer, joined women's professional teams overseas to get a chance to play professionally. Today, the professional women basketball players in the United States can play in two professional basketball leagues—the American Basketball League and the Women's National Basketball Association. Both are adding more teams each year. With interest in women's sports remaining high, the future for women's soccer and ice hockey also looks promising.

Playing professionally is not the only way to have a sports career. Perhaps you are interested in sports but not sure you can compete as an athlete. This is a realistic fear because there is only room for a certain number of professionals. But your experience as an athlete will help you in whatever career you choose. If you love sports, you should explore such careers as sport medicine, athletic training, sport psychology, sports agentry, team management, sport journalism, sport instruction, and coaching—all have opened up for women.

Women are increasing their sports participation in college and are making sports a part of their adult life for recreation, personal fitness, fun, and relaxation. This creates additional opportunities for sports instructors, coaches, fitness specialists, exercise trainers, and entrepreneurs who want to sell or deliver a sports product or service. A fast-growing area of employment for women in colleges and universities is the athletic department, where women are taking positions as athletic director, associate athletic director, and assistant athletic director.

Get Started Now

If you are wondering how to go about getting a job in sports or you want to explore careers in sports, this book is a good place to start. You'll find profiles of 10 women who love their work. You'll learn the duties and responsibilities that go with each job title, and you'll learn about the women themselves—what drew them to their work, how they found their first job, and how they took advantage of the opportunities that presented themselves.

Along with each profile you'll find a checklist with some clues about what type of person would be good in that particular job. There also is information about what salary you might expect to earn in jobs that are similar to the one described.

The last chapter, Getting Started on Your Own Career Path, gives advice about what to do now, suggests books to read, and lists organizations you may contact for additional information. As you think about a sports-related career, here are some ideas you should consider:

- When your school work requires research or projects where you select the topic, pick a sports topic that interests you.

- Read the sports pages of your local newspaper and *USA Today* to learn more about the world of sports.

- Read general sports magazines such as *Sports Illustrated* or magazines that cover your favorite sport, such as *Skiing*.

- Take courses related to sports and sports careers, such as biology, math, physical education, human anatomy, and health and fitness.

- Be sure you are well prepared for college. Most of the opportunities for sports careers depend on a college education and being involved in a college sports program.

- Volunteer in your areas of interest. If you want to be a coach, work with a kid's team at the city recreation department, for example. If you want to be a sports psychologist, volunteer at a sports clinic.

- Look for part-time employment working with any local sports team to learn about sports jobs from the inside.

- Don't be afraid to tell others about your interests and sports career goals and ask for their help. Seek out a mentor—someone you admire who works in a sport. Some of my most valuable experience and advice came from mentors who took an interest in me and what I wanted to accomplish.

- Take some business courses, such as business management or accounting if you are thinking about starting your own sports related business or working in an environment where you will have to manage a big budget.

- Never give up on your dream.

Whether or not you choose a career in sports, I encourage you to participate in team sports. Many successful women were members of sports teams as girls and young women. They learned, just as you will, the valuable lessons of teamwork—perseverance, tenacity, goal-setting, time management, fitness, and a healthy, confident self-image. You will find many challenges and the need to make tough choices as you participate in sports programs, but you also will reap the rewards of your hard work and develop friendships that can last a lifetime.

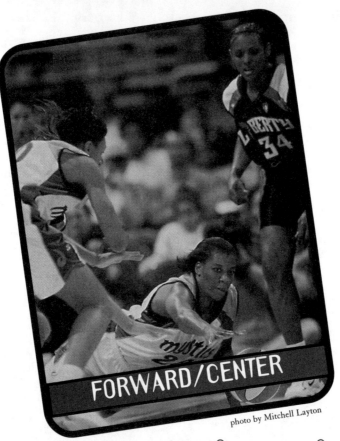

FORWARD/CENTER

photo by Mitchell Layton

Tammy Jackson

FORWARD/CENTER, Washington, DC, Mystics,
Women's National Basketball Association

Major in Recreation

Professional
Basketball Player

AT THE TOP OF HER GAME

Tammy Jackson started her career as a professional basketball player overseas, because there were no professional women's teams in 1984 in the United States. (American Basketball League, ABL, started in 1996; Women's National Basketball Association, WNBA, in 1997.) While in college, her coach encouraged her to "go professional" and helped her hire an agent who contacted teams and negotiated a contract for her.

Tammy's first contract was with a team in Sweden. She lived in Stockholm and played for them 3 years—the season ran August through April. Tammy spent May through July at home in Gainesville, FL.

"It was fun. I made many new friends and loved traveling. We went to Ger-

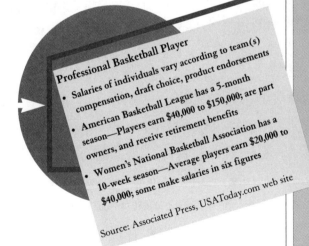

Professional Basketball Player
- Salaries of individuals vary according to team(s) compensation, draft choice, product endorsements
- American Basketball League has a 5-month season—Players earn $40,000 to $150,000; are part owners, and receive retirement benefits
- Women's National Basketball Association has a 10-week season—Average players earn $20,000 to $40,000; some make salaries in six figures

Source: Associated Press, USAToday.com web site

TAMMY'S CAREER PATH

Plays sports
with brothers

Plays
basketball in
high school

High scorer,
Lady Gators

many; Russia, and France for tournaments. I had never been overseas before. We won championships all three seasons." Tammy was the only American on the team and the only full-time professional, because the other women held jobs or attended school when they weren't playing. "They mix sports with their regular life. When I played with Italy's and Spain's teams, there were more professionals, although a lot of the women also went to school."

Tammy went to school in the summers to finish her degree in Recreation at University of Florida in Gainesville. Nowadays, she's playing almost year-round.

Day of the Game

Like most athletes, Tammy trains to keep fit. She has a personal trainer who works with her 3 days a week. The other days she works her conditioning program on various machines like the treadmill, stairmaster, and bicycle, and she lifts weights. Her trainer even had her pushing a car. Tammy runs in the early morning or in the cool of the evening to avoid the daytime heat of Florida.

On a day when there is a game (most are played around 8 in the evening), Tammy's morning is spent with the team. They practice shooting baskets and go over plays with the coach. "We work on getting our mind set for winning. We jump around a lot, sometimes joke with each other to help us relax."

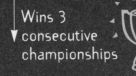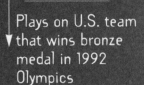
Around noon, Tammy goes home. She may run a few errands, but usually relaxes to get her mind off the game. She eats a light meal of pasta or chicken, takes a nap, talks to friends, and watches television. At 6 o'clock she is back at the locker room where the music is loud and festive. During the next hour she'll see family and fans, then relax in the whirlpool, getting her body ready for the game. About an hour before the game, the team goes on the court to shoot a few baskets and talk with reporters. Then, a pastor gives a devotional service for those players who want to attend. "These quiet moments for getting in touch with your spiritual side are very important to me." About 30 minutes to game time, the coach goes over strategy and the players head out for the court and warm up. After the game, win or lose, there is a pep talk from the coach and players get the schedule for the next couple of days. Then Tammy has a shower, may go out for dinner, then it's home and bedtime.

"I love the game of basketball. If that love ever leaves me, I'll stop playing. There's so much to the game. I like the strategy, playing offensive, learning what my teammates like and don't like, what kind of passes they like. There's a lot to basketball other than just running up and down the court and shooting baskets."

Joins Houston
▼ Comets, wins
WNBA championship

Joins Washington, D.C.,
▼ Mystics

Career Highlights

Tammy finished her University of Florida's Lady Gators career averaging 17.1 points and 10.3 rebounds per game. She played three seasons with Solna, Sweden, and three with Shizuoka, Japan, which she led to three consecutive championships. She was a member of the bronze-medal-winning U.S. Olympic Team in 1992. She led the Italian league in steals in 1995-96. She split the 1996-1997 season between Cesena, Italy and Limoges, France, and averaged 15.8 points and

If you want to do a sport, don't let anyone tell you you can't do it. People may say you're not good enough, or girls can't do that.

11 rebounds a game for Limoges. She was selected by WNBA's Houston Comets, April 1997, in the second round. Houston won the WNBA Championship, and Tammy posted 7 points and a team-high 11 rebounds in a 65-51 win over the New York Liberty team in the winning game in August 1997.

The summer season that Houston won the championship, "We celebrated at the arena locker room for about 2 hours afterward, yelling, hugging each other. We were at our home court and our families joined us. It was great. Then we all went our separate ways. All 3 years when the Swedish team won, we were away from home court. So the team celebrated together—we went out to eat together and the next morning continued to celebrate as we traveled home together. It was quite special."

In April 1998, Tammy was drafted by the Washington, DC, Mystics, where she will play forward or center.

CAREER CHECKLIST ✓

You'll like this job if you ...

Love to compete in basketball

Are disciplined and tenacious

Are courageous and determined to be a top athlete

Are confident and believe in yourself

GROUNDBREAKERS

In a segregated United States in 1916, African Americans created the American Tennis Association. The first national championships took place in Baltimore in 1917. Lucy B. Stowe, a Baltimore native, won the women's singles title and became the first Black woman athletic champion.

source: Contributions of Black Women to America Vol II. (1982). Marianna W. Davis Ed.

Brotherly Love

Tammy was born and raised in Gainesville. The youngest of six children, she has one sister and four brothers. Growing up, she spent a lot of time with her brothers outdoors playing basketball and touch football, and running together. "I was a tomboy. Guess I should have known I'd be an athlete, but I didn't."

Tammy didn't play basketball at school until high school. "When I got to Buchholt High School, my brothers told me I was going to play basketball. They had already told the coach about me." Tammy not only played basketball all 4 years, she also played 3 years of volleyball and did 1 year of track. Standing 6 foot 2 inches, Tammy said her height was no problem for her. "There were lots of tall boys in my school. Everyone knew me and my family, we're all tall."

While Tammy knew she would go to college, she didn't plan on playing basketball there. But when she was a junior, the coach from the University of Florida talked with her and Tammy started

photo by Mitchell Layton

thinking about it. A small university in Alabama also was interested in having her play, but after visiting the campus, Tammy knew she didn't want to go away from her home in Gainesville. So she went to the University of Florida.

Tammy was leading scorer her first year with the Lady Gators. "I wanted to be the best college player I could. I could have worked harder to improve parts of my game, but at that time I didn't see any future in being a professional player." But that changed in her junior year when she learned there were women's professional teams overseas that she could try out for.

You can make time for a job or school work and do a sport. Get your grades so you'll be able to get to college.

There are people out there
who might want to
use you because of
your ability,
so you need to know about
the world and you can
learn much from studying.
But if you make
mistakes,
learn from them and
go on.

Strong Role Models

During her school years, Tammy had a lot of family support. "They came to my games. They encouraged me. As long as I had my school work done, everything was fine with my parents."

Tammy calls herself a strong-minded woman. "When I decide to do something, I do it. I am appreciative of the strong coaches that helped me. Starting with Billie Green in high school, and in college Mickie DeMoss and Debbie Yow. All those women had an idea of what they wanted to do in their life and they did it. Growing up I'd seen a lot of coaches in sports, but they were all men. I was lucky to know these women who were so happy doing what they were doing."

Tammy is a spiritually minded woman. The first time she left home and went to Sweden, "I took God with me. I put my faith in God. If you have something you definitely believe in spiritually, it helps you. Sometime things go wrong, maybe you just don't get to start the game, or you don't feel like working hard, or there may be a crisis in the family. It helps me to have a quiet time with God."

Tammy owns her own home in Gainesville, which her Dad lives in and takes care of while she's away playing ball. Someday, Tammy would like to marry and have children. For now, when she's home she works with children ages 9 to 15 in the city's recreation program. "There are lots of distractions out there—drugs, things that look like easy money. Kids need to learn to say no to things that might deter them from their dreams of what they want to do. They need to be strong. People may say you're not good enough, or girls can't do that, but there is time to do it if you're disciplined."

GOLF PROFESSIONAL

Julieta Stack

GOLF PROFESSIONAL, Capitol City Golf School at East Potomac G
Club, Washington, DC
OWNER AND PRESIDENT, **InnerDrive Inc.** Washington, DC

Major in International Relations

Golf
Professional

IT TAKES DRIVE TO SUCCEED

The golf course is her favorite place. During the past 9 years, Julieta Stack has spent as much time as possible there, playing golf and teaching. She gives private and group lessons, she practices her own game, she competes in various playing events. Julieta also helps people select golf clubs that are suitable in weight and height and is a certified Ping golf club fitter. (She helps people select clubs that fit their hands, height, and strength.) This past year she formed her own company, InnerDrive, Inc.

On a typical weekend day at Washington, DC's East Potomac golf course, Julieta will start about 8 in the morning and give one-on-one private lessons. She describes the work as mental. "I watch closely to analyze the golfer. You have to

Golf Professional
- $12,000 to $125,000
- Private and group lessons—40% or more of rate charged
- Earnings from selling equipment, running pro shop

Source: Career Opportunities in the Sports Industry by Shelly Field. (1991).

JULIETA'S CAREER PATH

Lives next to
▼ golf course

Basketball and track in high
▼ school

Track scholarsh
▼ Florida college

get into the person's head and figure what they are thinking that gets them into that position, that movement. Then you can teach them how to correct those wrong moves."

From 9 a.m. to 1 p.m. there are the golf school classes. "Here you need energy and enthusiasm to explain and demonstrate. The groups can be as large as 15 people. I feel like it's showtime for me." After that she will give more private lessons. Then there may be time for Julieta to get out on the course and play 9 holes or hit practice balls. In the busiest part of the summer in Washington, instructors usually go nonstop from 8 to 6. They don't have much time or energy to play golf except during a day off.

When the summer season is over, Julieta may play in a fall tournament, then head south and work at a course in Florida for the winter. She may play in

another event before returning to East Potomac Golf Club in the spring.

Julieta is a member of the Ladies Professional Golf Association (LPGA) Teaching and Club Professional Division. That means she has met all the requirements and is certified by the LPGA to teach. She is also a member advisor of LPGA and counsels new instructors.

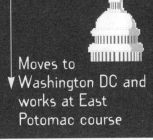

Moves to Washington DC and works at East Potomac course

After graduates, works at and plays golf

Gets LPGA instructor certified

A Blend of Fitness and Golf Instruction

Julieta formed her own company to offer her special learning techniques to a wider audience. She specializes in holding teaching clinics and seminars, and in arranging golf outings. Julieta is a fitness instructor certified by the National Sports Performance Association. She has created an innovative blend of fitness instruction along with golf instruction to help golfers swing the clubs effectively. The exercises help people increase club head speed and hit the proper spot where the club impacts the ball. Julieta offers her golf program to local sport and health clubs. Her company also arranges golf travel for small groups of varying ability levels.

"It is difficult to master the mechanics of the golf swing. But the motions are quite similar to things we do in every day life. I get students to recall some of these familiar movements. We swing a bat, toss a ball overhand, play Frisbee. The younger women pick it up quickly. But women who didn't get the opportunity to play sports in school have more trouble. When I taught Pat Schroeder (former U. S. Representative, Democrat, from Colorado), she was doing this strange wrist movement. When I tried to get her to 'recall' other sports, she said, 'I've

JULIETA'S CAREER PATH

gets physical
▼ fitness certified

Starts own
▼ business InnerDrive

never played any other sport.' That means I have to find other moves these women might know that will relate to the golf swing."

A Seasonal Game

In the North, golf is a seasonal game that can't be played on snow and ice. It is year round in the South and southwestern USA. Tournament activity is also year round and global. Julieta went to play in the French Open in September 1997, her first overseas event. "I missed the cut (persons wanting to compete must be among the top scorers in qualifying rounds in order to play in the event.), but it was the most fascinating experience that I've ever had in golf. I went

and played in Scotland all by myself. I had my clubs and a small travel bag. The clubs are like an ice breaker for people. No matter where I go, even on vacation, I pull the clubs out and I might as well call it home. I've been to so many courses up and down the East Coast, and there are no barriers of age, race, or gender." Next, Julieta is looking at qualifying for the Australian Open.

Julieta's Dad an Avid Golfer

From age 6 to 11, Julieta lived in Brigantine, NJ, next to a golf course. Her mother and father both played, but her Dad was the avid golfer. "I'd spend hours hanging around the club house, waiting for my Dad. It was great. And I'd go out anytime and play just a few holes near the house."

Julieta didn't play golf during high school. Her school had one of the top-ranked basketball programs. She played basketball and did almost everything in track events. At graduation, Julieta got a partial scholarship for track. She attended Florida State University in Tallahassee for 2 years. "It was the time of the summer Olympics in Los Angeles. There must have been at least eight athletes at FSU who were Olympians; quite a few won medals. Training with them taught me that the work ethic had to be there to succeed, but it could be acquired through discipline, desire, and hard work. I was never a star, but I could hustle, and I was known for being a hard worker. I found I could accomplish quite a bit just through hard work."

After completing 2 years of basic courses, Julieta decided she wanted to major in international studies, an area she'd been interested in for some time. She transferred to American University in Washington, DC. At her first school break, Julieta planned on visiting her

CAREER CHECKLIST ✓

You'll like this job if you ...

Have a love of golf

Have a tremendous amount of patience

Like to teach

Will work hard to be a good athlete

Don't be afraid to ask people for guidance. They are not going to come to you. You have to ask.

Dad. Her parents had divorced, and he had moved to Atlanta.

"I was determined to rekindle the bond with my Dad, but I knew he had a low level of tolerance for golfers who were not very good. So I took 'Golf 101' at the University. It didn't work. Dad tried to give me a couple lessons, but it was frustrating to us both. So he took me to his pro, and got me set up. Then he left. That was best thing he could have done. It was great—no frustration and no pressure from Dad watching me. It was just me and the pro. I think that holds true for kids of any age. It's nice for parents to be there on the periphery, to support you, but there's extra pressure if the parent is there all the time watching. It creates an anxiety, an added burden."

When Julieta came back from that vacation, her college studies were going well, but she missed being outdoors. She decided she would get a job at a driving range, and the closest one was East Potomac. They hired her immediately. She rode her bike to work (about 7 miles each way). "It was great. I got to hit all the balls I wanted. The people working there were good golfers and they gave me tips. I had the ideal learning situation. What I do when I want to learn something is immerse myself in it, go nuts with it. That way, either you'll figure out this is not what you're up to, or you really do have

the skill for it. I just had this bug, I can't really explain it."

When Julieta graduated, she was undecided whether she wanted to continue her studies to get a master's degree, or work in International Relations, or go to law school. She wanted some "thinking time" to figure out what she really wanted to do. She planned a long visit with her father in Atlanta. When she got to town, she drove around the area, found a golf course, and asked for a job. "I wanted a place to practice and play without it costing me a lot of money."

Julieta worked at Sugar Creek Golf Course. "It was wonderful. I met the greatest people there. After few months, I went to Florida, played events, and picked up odd jobs here and there. I found I just didn't want to go back to school."

Julieta decided to pursue golf and started playing in amateur tournaments. Since she wasn't sponsored and didn't come from a wealthy family, she had to find jobs working at various places where she could get paid, but also could practice and play golf. Once she took a job as grounds crew in Largo, FL. "We'd have

GROUNDBREAKERS

Called "the greatest woman athlete of all time," Mildred Ella Didrikson Zaharias (1911-1956) started organized sports as a basketball player on a company team, averaging 42 points per game. In the 1932 Olympics, she was the best track athlete in the world—in one day she won the 80-meter hurdles, baseball throw, long jump, shot put, and javelin thrown, and tied for first in the high jump. In golf, she founded the Ladies Professional Golf Association. She competed professionally for 8 years and won 31 LPGA tournaments.

Source: Great Women Athletes of the 20th Century

to rake bunkers by hand. It took hours in the hot sun, and you only got paid minimum wage. But I stayed until I could get to the next level."

Tour Play and Teaching

Julieta wanted to get in the LPGA tour, but to do that she needed a job that paid more money, so she applied to the LPGA teaching program. "Teaching at $20 per half hour was much better than working jobs at minimum wage." Her application was accepted and she began attending classes and workshops that stressed teaching but also discussed the business end of being a golf instructor. "I watched other instructors teach. That was so valuable to me. I'd go up to a pro and ask if I could observe for 30 minutes. These days people in the program have a mentor who helps out."

To get certified, applicants must take a written test and practical exam, as well as have a good playing score (85 or less for 18 holes). In the practical exam, applicants

All through my career I've
reached out to
other people for guidance.
The worst thing anyone
ever said to me was
"No, I can't help you."
I find people are very
willing to help you if you
come to them with the
right attitude.

At college, I was never a star, but I could hustle, and I was known for being a hard worker. I found I could accomplish quite a bit just through hard work.

teach three people the full swing and the short game—people they've never seen before. It takes about 4 years to get the top Class A certification. All pros must get recertification points to keep their certification. "You can't rest on your laurels; you always have to be educating yourself. I like that, and the LPGA is very supportive."

Playing Highlights

There are two events during the year that help players qualify for the LPGA tour and get the coveted tour card—tournaments in California and Florida. The top one-third from each event advance to the finals, held in Daytona, FL, in October. At the qualifying finals players compete against all of the tour players who didn't earn enough money in the previous season to keep their tour cards and players no longer exempt from competition. Only the top 20 or so get LPGA Tour Cards. Julieta was a LPGA Tour Qualifying finalist in 1992.

Teaching allowed Julieta to compete, although not on the same level as tour players. And she didn't have a sponsor. Here are her playing highlights from 1990 to 1997:

- Julieta was a member of Central Florida Challenge Women's Professional Tour (1990-94, 1997).
- 1994 Winner Women's Middle Atlantic Washington Golf Magazine Pro-Am.

- Ten Top-Ten finishes in professional events since 1992.
- Alternate in two U.S. Women's Open events.

Today Julieta is spending a bit more time indoors as she works at her new business. When she gets leisure time, she attends operas, plays, and other events.

"Being a golf pro is one of the healthiest lifestyles. And pros are the happiest people I've ever been with. We share how hard we've had to work, and how we're teaching. It's fun. The games, the courses, these are like snapshots in your head that will never go away. Golf crosses all the lines—age, gender, race. Any person can play. I love it."

DIRECTOR

Mary Beth Quinn

DIRECTOR, Wintergreen Resort Ski and Snowboard School, VA

Ski & Snowboard
Instructor

SNOW SENSE

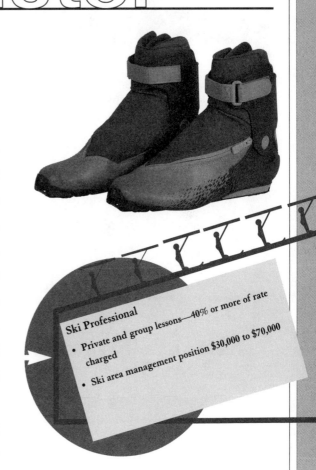

Ski Professional
- Private and group lessons—40% or more of rate charged
- Ski area management position $30,000 to $70,000

Mary Beth Quinn believes that to ski is one of the most wonderful things in the world. She thinks snow skiing should be enjoyed by people of all ages and all incomes. That's why she's working so hard to make Wintergreen Resort, outside Charlottesville, VA, a place where kids, teenagers, adult women and men, and senior citizens will all enjoy skiing and snowboarding.

Mary Beth, who loves teaching skiing as much as anything in life except her two children, is the director of the ski and snowboard school at Wintergreen. She oversees a staff of more than 130 instructors. In addition to the school, Mary Beth manages the children's ski and snowboard programs, a ski academy for college students, the junior race team, school

MARY BETH'S CAREER PATH

Chosen for Burke
▼ Mountain Academy

Skis on the national ski team

Enters the Unive
▼ of Vermont to st
clothing design

programs, and special events. In the summer, she also promotes the idea of skiing at Wintergreen.

Recently, Mary Beth created a program for women who are just learning to ski. "I'm very interested in helping Moms learn how to keep up when the family goes skiing," she says. "Often Dad is fearless and the kids are too young to be afraid, so Mom, the sensible one, sometimes gets left behind on the slopes. The way we teach, she can take her time in

In the winter, my training was mostly skiing, but in the summer training consisted of physical exercises such as weight lifting, biking, and running.

Designs her own
▼ line of ski knitwear
called Snowear

Opens retail clothing
▼ stores

Marries,
▼ has two children

learning in a supportive environment and develop the skills she needs so that the whole family can ski together."

Mary Beth's dream is to make Wintergreen the best place to ski in the Southeastern United States. She wants great programs and first class slopes where there is room for all the different age groups to learn. Wintergreen is different from many other ski resorts that are owned by a company to make a profit. Wintergreen is a member-owned resort community. Members pay dues to use the facilities, including the ski slopes, two 18-hole and one 9-hole golf courses, indoor and outdoor tennis courts, swimming pools, spa, hiking trails, boating, and about anything else you could

imagine doing in the mountains. The ski facilities also are open to large groups and individual day visitors who want to buy a lift ticket. To get more people to the slopes, Mary Beth has created programs for beginners, women, seniors, and children.

Skiing In Stowe, Vermont

When Mary Beth was in the second grade, her parents moved from New York to Stowe, VT, where there is some of the best skiing in the United States. On Friday afternoon, school kids would be bused to the mountain to ski. It was part of their school curriculum! Kids could also ski free on either Saturday or Sunday.

MARY BETH'S CAREER PATH

Teaches skiing
▼ at Wintergreen
Resort

Becomes director of the
▼ Wintergreen ski school

Mary Beth's parents would take her and her two brothers to the slopes every weekend during ski season. A paper bag lunch and a quarter for a candy bar and a drink would provide the nourishment for the day. The kids would ski the mountain until three o'clock.

At 12 years old, Mary Beth was diagnosed with scoliosis, or curvature of the spine, a problem she was born with. The doctors put her into a Milwaukee brace that went from her neck to her hips to try to correct the curvature. But one doctor said that sports would strengthen her back and she didn't have to wear the brace when she was engaged in sports activity. To escape being in the brace all the time, Mary Beth became a super jock. It was natural she would gravitate toward skiing. She was very good. By the time she was in the eighth grade, she was only wearing the brace at night.

Because she was such a good skier, she was selected for a school in the Northeast Kingdom (corner) of Vermont called Burke Mountain Academy. The school was the first in-residence school to train athletes for the national ski team. Students lived at the school on the side of a mountain, studying half the day and training half the day. School consisted of independent study. In the winter, training was mostly skiing, but in the summer training consisted of physical exercises such as weight lifting, biking and running. To support her in her efforts to ski competitively, her father bought a 350-acre farm near the school and moved the whole family there.

Mary Beth was a good enough skier to travel with the national ski team and to ski all over the United States. She was aiming for the Olympics. But by the time she was 17, she was tired. To ski competi-

tively you have to give up everything and stay completely focused on skiing. After a couple of bad accidents, Mary Beth finally decided that she did not want to ski competitively anymore. She had lost the drive.

Instead, in her senior year of high school, she began teaching skiing at Burke Mountain. She found that she loved teaching skiing even more than she had loved competitive skiing. She knew she had made the right choice. "Many of my peers who worked so hard to ski competitively don't even ski anymore because they got so burned out," she says. "But here I am, still skiing at 41 years old."

From Skis to Skiwear

When she graduated from the Academy, Mary Beth enrolled at the University of Vermont as a Clothing, Textiles, and Design major. She wanted to be a skiwear designer. She raced on the school ski team for a little while, decided she didn't really enjoy racing anymore, and began

GROUNDBREAKERS

Ann Bancroft was the first woman to travel across the ice to the North Pole and the first woman to travel across Greenland on skis.
In 1993, she was the leader of the American Women's Expedition, a group of four who skied more than 600 miles to the South Pole.

teaching and coaching skiing at the University. But at college, Mary Beth lost some of the discipline she had learned as an athlete. Her spinal curvature got worse, and the doctors urged her to have an operation. When she couldn't stand the pain any longer, she took her doctors' advice and had an operation called a spinal fusion. Doctors grafted a piece of bone from her hip to her spine and put a steel rod in her back to straighten her spine. She had to spend an entire year in a body cast.

Mary Beth had to leave school. She moved back to the farmhouse to live with her parents and her two brothers. She couldn't do much physically except to take a short walk with her dogs each day, but she read a tremendous amount and thought about her future. Her father, who always told her she could accomplish anything she wanted if she set her mind to it, encouraged her to work on designing knit ski hats. He worked for a well-known manufacturer of ski equipment, and he had the connections to develop a sales force if she could deliver the samples. He bought her a knitting machine, and Mary Beth spent the year while she was recuperating developing "Snowear."

The first selling season was a huge success! Before she was even out of the body cast, she had moved to Burlington, VT,

to include sweaters. She contracted with two mills, one in New Hampshire, and one in Massachusetts, to knit the sweaters she had designed. But the mills cut the sweaters wrong and didn't deliver on

purchased a large quantity of wool which was lighter and more natural looking than most ski hats at the time, and contracted with 25 women to knit the hats in their homes on their own knitting machines. The business took off the first 2 years, and Mary Beth expanded her line

time, so Mary Beth couldn't fill the orders she had promised. She opened a retail ski clothing store in Burlington to sell the sweaters. Her first store did well, but when Mary Beth expanded to a second store, she had grown too fast too soon and had to sell the business. "I have learned a lot in the school of hard knocks," she says. "It's a good teacher about what it's really like to own your own business."

A Family Role

By this time she was 26 years old, and Mary Beth felt like she had done as much as most 50-year-olds. She had competed and skied all over the world, had created and managed two businesses, and had become a fully certified ski instructor. About this time she decided to get married to a real estate broker she had been dating for years. They settled in Burlington and she worked part-time helping in his real estate office and continuing to teach in Stowe in the winter.

But the couple didn't stay in Vermont. After the birth of her two daughters, Lara, now 8, and Anna, now 6, Mary Beth and her husband moved to the South. Eventually the family ended up in Charlottesville, VA, where, Mary Beth says, her life consisted of going to the gym to work out and the grocery store to buy diapers for the baby. She loved her girls more than anything in the world, but she felt cut off from the life she had known before, full of skiing and running a business. When the director of the ski school at Wintergreen asked her to teach skiing there part time, she rejoiced at the idea of working again.

It took Mary Beth 5 years to become the director of the ski school. She loves to teach, but running the school is even more challenging. Currently, she's in the process of working with the ski area manager to develop the ski slopes so there is enough room to teach beginner kids and adults how to ski on relatively flat land. At most ski areas, you take a lift to the top of the mountain and ski down. Lessons can be given at the bottom of the mountain. But at Wintergreen Resort, you are already at the top of the mountain that you ski down, and there isn't much flat area on top for lessons. Mary Beth has already put in some terraced areas where ski lessons can be given. This way people can practice and learn before they have to go down the mountain.

In the winter, Mary Beth works long days, driving down the mountain to her home in Charlottesville to arrive home at 7:00 p.m. or later after an hour's commute. On the weekends, she rents a condo at Wintergreen and stays there because her day starts at 7 a.m. and doesn't end until 9 p.m. or later. She would rather spend more time with her girls right now, but she and her husband divorced a few years ago, and Mary Beth needs to earn a living to support herself and her children.

Her mother has moved in with her and helps take care of the girls. Mary Beth knows that her girls respect her work, and they love to ski too. When they come to the resort on the weekends, they always tell everyone their Mom is the boss of the ski school. "Being the school director at Wintergreen combines a challenging career with the pleasure of working and raising a family in beautiful surroundings.

SPORTS JOURNALIST AND
BROADCASTER

Robin Roberts

SPORTS JOURNALIST AND BROADCASTER, **ESPN and ABC** Television
Major in Communications

Sports Broadcaster

ON-CAMERA PIONEER IN A MAN'S WORLD

Robin Roberts rises early on Friday morning and reads the sports pages of various city papers and national magazines. A couple of hours later a chauffeur-driven car picks her up at her home in a Connecticut suburb and takes her into Manhattan for an early morning breakfast sponsored by one of her employers, ESPN TV Sports Network. She follows this with a lunch and business meeting at ABC's Wide World of Sports, also an employer. Then she attends a sports banquet on behalf of tennis pro Arthur Ashe in New York City, after which she flies to Reno, NV, to speak at an awards banquet for college athletes. On Saturday she is back in New York for another meeting, and then a broadcast for ABC's Wide World of Sports. On Sun-

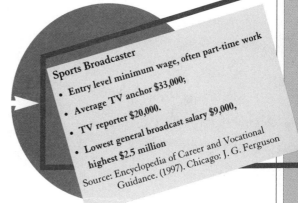

Sports Broadcaster
- Entry level minimum wage, often part-time work
- Average TV anchor $33,000;
- TV reporter $20,000.
- Lowest general broadcast salary $9,000, highest $2.5 million

Source: Encyclopedia of Career and Vocational Guidance. (1997). Chicago: J. G. Ferguson

ROBIN'S CAREER PATH

Plays basketball, tennis, and works on yearbook

Graduates salutatorian, gets sports scholarship

Plays basketball, covers sports for campus radio

day, her feature on a successful Texas businessman runs on television's Good Morning America Sunday.

One of the most visible women in sports journalism, Robin is also one of the most versatile. She is a play-by-play commentator for Women's National Basketball Association games, hosts ABC Wide World of Sports, hosts an ESPN SportsLight, prime time TV interview program; anchors ESPN SportsCenter major events like Wimbledon, and is the primary reporter and host for ESPN's coverage of the Winter and Summer Olympics. In the early 1990s, she was a part of NFL PrimeTime, an interview show about football. She has hosted ESPN's coverage of the National Collegiate Athletic Association (NCAA) women's finals, the NCAA Women's Basketball Tournament, and LPGA golf tournaments. Recently, she took on a new challenge doing feature stories and serving as co-host for the ABC-TV show Good Morning America Sunday.

"These days I don't limit what I want to do," Robin says. "I like doing news as well as sports, but it's got to be human interest stories. I like using stories to illustrate certain principles about life."

Behind the Camera

When Robin first started in TV sports journalism, she not only did the reporting, she wrote the scripted material, carried the video camera to shoot the action, edited the video, and edited the story to fit the 4 or 5 minutes she was given. "Some young people think all you have to do is to get in front of the camera and talk, but that's only a small part of it. You have to have good writing skills and know how to communicate through both film and words." As she became more well

I played sports from a young age. It teaches you teamwork, confidence, focus, and follow through—all qualities which are necessary for success.

ROBIN'S CAREER PATH

Hosts ABC's Wide World of Sports

Does features for TV's Good Morning America Sunday

known, Robin didn't have to worry about lugging a camera around, but she still has to do a good part of the writing for sports programs, especially when she is anchoring or hosting a show.

Her favorite work is live coverage of sports events. "There is an electricity about live broadcasts that you just don't get in delayed broadcasting. You never know what's going to happen next and that's exciting. It can be dangerous; you don't want to embarrass yourself in broadcasting an event, so you have to think fast and edit in your head as you go along."

The hardest thing about being a woman sports broadcaster, says Robin, is that you have to prove to both network executives and the people who watch sports programs that you know a lot about sports. You also have to be very good at what you do. While men broad-

casters can make a mistake and then laugh it off, a woman who seems not to know what she's talking about will have a tough time finding acceptance in the world of sports journalism. "In one of my first jobs on television, a man called up before I'd even had my first show and said he didn't like the idea of my doing the sports because I was a woman," Robin says. "I asked him to give me a chance and at least wait until he'd heard me before he decided I couldn't do it. He called back a few months later and said he really liked the way I covered the sports news."

A College Athlete and Broadcaster

Robin spent much of her youth in Biloxi, MS, where her father, who flew with the first group of black military pilots, the Tuskagee Airmen, was stationed. She is the youngest of four children.

She has been interested in sports for as long as she can remember. At 12, she was a state bowling champion. In high school she played basketball and tennis, and her first ambition was to be a professional athlete. A salutatorian of her Pass Christian 1979 graduating class, she got her first journalism experience working on the high school yearbook. Her older sister, Sally Ann, a professional news journalist TV anchor/reporter, let Robin tag along sometimes when she was working, and Robin got a taste of the real world of journalism.

After high school Robin accepted a scholarship to Southeastern Louisiana University. It was the only school that would award her a scholarship in both tennis and basketball. She didn't want to have to choose between the two sports. But once she was on campus, she understood that she would have to concentrate on one sport or the other. She chose basketball, ending her career as the school's third all-time leading scorer (1,446

CAREER CHECKLIST ✓

You'll like this job if you ...

Like to write and can speak well

Love sports

Are inquisitive and willing to learn about many different subjects

Are willing to start at the bottom and work hard for low pay

GROUNDBREAKERS

When First Lady Bess Truman was 13 years old and walking to dance class in a dress and pumps, she passed an all-boy baseball game. Her brothers were on the losing side, which had managed to fill the bases in the last inning. Tapped to pinch-hit, she slugged a home run, winning the game. She commented, "It would be a poor kind of sister that wouldn't help a brother in need."

SOURCE: What Women Have Done calendar, Library of Congress.

points) and rebounder (1,034). She anchored sports news programs on her campus radio station, and provided play-by-play coverage of many college games.

In college, Robin discovered she had broad and varied interests, but not the single-mindedness to be a professional athlete. In her sophomore year, she decided to major in journalism, knowing that sports journalism would keep her close to the world of sports that she loved so much.

After graduation she landed that first sports job, which paid $5.50 per hour for a 30-hour week. She was a weekend sports anchor at a local radio station. Her teachers, friends, and parents tried to convince her to try news reporting because it paid better, but Robin, true to her own interests, stuck to the sports reporting. When she applied for a job at a Nashville TV station and got it, it was evident she was passionate about sports. She became a member of the TV sports team.

RECORDING

The Men's World of Sports

When she joined ESPN in 1990, Robin had to convince a national public that a woman could do sports reporting competently. It didn't take long for her to gain the respect and admiration of her audience. She spent 5 years on the sports highlights show NFL PrimeTime. She never had problems with the athletes accepting her despite her gender. Because she also had been an athlete, she could understand their world and they respected her for it. But it was courageous of ESPN to place her in such a high visibility position. There just hadn't been that many female sports broadcast journalists when she started her television career.

"I was able to overcome the odds against a woman sports journalist because of my family's support and my upbringing," Robin says. "My father was one of the first black men who had the opportunity to fly an airplane, and my family was always there and always supportive when I was young. It also helped that I played sports from a young age. It

Whatever you think you want to do, find somebody who is good at it and then contact them. Ask them questions about what their work is like and find out if it is for you. Get as much information as you can about what skills are required and how you get the knowledge and experience you need.

teaches you teamwork, confidence, focus, and follow through, all qualities which are necessary for success."

Robin is proud that she has been a voice to help women's basketball gain more visibility. "Early in my career, I did pretty much strictly men's sports. People came to know me and trust me as an authority on sports. So when I started covering women's basketball, lots of people who might not have tuned in were attracted to the game. People are just beginning to appreciate women's basketball. It's a different game than men's basketball. It's not so flashy, but when the games are good, it is some of the best basketball being played today."

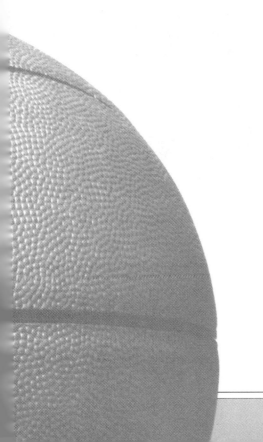

DIRECTOR OF ATHLETICS

Deborah A. Yow

DIRECTOR OF ATHLETICS, **University of Maryland**, College Park

Major in English; Master of Arts, Human Behavior/Counseling; Doctorate, Human Behavior/Counseling

Athletic Director

CHARGED UP AND IN CHARGE

Deborah Yow is the athletic director of the University of Maryland, a top-rated, Division I university in the Atlantic Coast Conference. She is the top executive of the university's athletic program. Her job is to see that everything runs smoothly—that the athletes pass their academic courses, that the coaches improve the athletes' performances, that the teams win more than they lose, and that athletes and coaches have what they need to be successful.

In a typical week, Debbie will work 55 hours or more (40 hours in the summer) running the organization that covers 24 sports, 600 student athletes, and 140 employees.

Every day she talks to newspaper or broadcast people. It could be answering

Athletic Director
- High school $25,000 to $50,000
- Small college $28,000 to $60,000
- Large university $90,000 to $250,000

Chose basketball over cheerleading

Taught and coached at high school

Full-time women coach at U of Kentucky

their questions about a new coach, or explaining a new building plan, or announcing a big money gift for the athletic program.

She also negotiates radio and television contracts to broadcast the University's games. These contracts contribute to the athletic program's $27 million budget. That money, which must be raised each year, goes toward athletic scholarships, all the traveling the teams do, and their equipment. It pays the coaches, the administrative staff, and other employees. The State funds from taxpayers can only be spent for things like the University's buildings that athletes use. Individuals make donations and the fan (or booster) organizations raise lots of money for the athletic program.

The first year Debbie had her job, she overhauled a debt-ridden athletic department and balanced the budget for the first time in 10 years, and she continues to balance the budgets. Among her many achievements: she expanded the fund-raising staff and donations increased. She increased academic support for athletes and graduation rates improved to above that of the general student body. She made the department proactive in complying with regulations—institutional, conference, and NCAA rules and Title IX mandates. "It is a complex job, sometimes overwhelming, but I love it."

Met Bill at Oral
▼ Roberts U

Became fund
▼ raiser for
Florida Gators

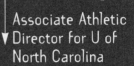
Associate Athletic
▼ Director for U of
North Carolina

Coaching the Coaches

A big part of Debbie's job is "coaching" the coaches. The football and men's basketball coaches report directly to her; and monthly she meets with the entire coaching staff. Her years of coaching college women's basketball help her. "We're part of the same group. There's a special feeling we have for each other because we've 'been there, done that.' Coaching is teaching. Coaches have great opportunities to profoundly impact the lives of young people. There is a special relationship between player and coach."

Debbie attends lots of sports events and is part of the official travel group going to the away games. She meets with many groups, belongs to several organizations, and often is a featured speaker.

She's Cute

When Debbie was in junior high, she was a cheerleader and majorette, in addition to playing sports. At a seventh grade softball game, she and her girl friend quietly moved into the stands to sit behind a boy that Debbie was interested in. They overheard him say to a friend, "I think Debbie's cute." "Yeah," said the other boy, "too bad she plays softball." Upset, Debbie later asked her parents what was wrong with girls who played softball.

"They assured me that I could do whatever I wanted; it wouldn't make me less feminine. It was the boy's problem, they said. That stuck with me, and whenever I ran into that attitude, I'd say, 'well, that's his problem.'" One time in college, Debbie was playing handball with her boy friend, a football player, and beating him. He got angrier and angrier, but she wasn't going to lose on purpose just to please him. "I thought 'that's his problem.' On the first date with my future husband, Bill, we shot baskets playing Horse, and he beat me. I rarely lost at Horse, and I was impressed."

The Famous Yow Sisters

Debbie grew up in Gibonsville, in the Piedmont area of North Carolina, where sports were a big part of community life. Adults played on teams sponsored by local businesses, and school boys and girls played on teams, competing throughout Gilford County. Everyone knew Debbie's cousin Virgil Yow. "In the 1950s, at High Point College, he placed a woman on the men's college basketball team he was coaching. That was unheard of, but he did it because she was an outstanding player. He told her to just shoot the basket and then get out of the way so she wouldn't get hurt. But she ignored him, followed the shot to the board, and did fine."

All the Yow women enjoy sports. Debbie's mother played in an adult league on a company-sponsored basketball team back in 1939. Debbie's older sister, Kay, is head coach at North Carolina State in Chapel Hill. Her younger sister, Susan, is assistant coach of the Cleveland Rockers, a WNBA (Women's National Basketball Association) team. They have had articles written about them in magazines like *Sports Illustrated*. (February, 1977).

At high school Debbie had to choose between cheerleading or playing basketball. She couldn't do both. She played basketball and softball throughout high school. "Girls were 'allowed' to play basketball starting in seventh grade. We had a team that traveled with the boys' team. We had double headers, so where they went, we went. The girls played first, then the boys. I didn't realize that wasn't the norm for all schools."

Debbie planned to make her career in teaching and started college at East Carolina. She transferred to Elon College, where her sister Kay had just become women's coach and they were

CAREER CHECKLIST ✓

You'll like this job if you ...

Can juggle many different projects at the same time

Accept responsibility, but can delegate

Enjoy a challenge and play to win

Can communicate, both speaking and writing

Coaching is teaching. Coaches have great opportunities to profoundly impact the lives of young people. There is a special relationship between player and coach.

forming a women's basketball program. Debbie played on Elon's basketball team, coached a junior high girls' team, worked part-time jobs to pay for school, and graduated with a major in English.

A Love of Coaching

Debbie's first full-time job was teaching high school English and coaching girls' basketball at a high school. "I thought that's what I would do the rest of my life." But a brochure Debbie happened to pick up at the University of North Carolina, where she was applying for graduate school, changed her life. "The University of Kentucky was going to hire its first full-time women's basketball coach. This was 1976. I had never heard of anything like that and thought what an interesting idea. I remembered Kentucky because Elon had played them, but I really knew nothing about the University. I applied for and got the job. My parents were shocked that I would leave North Carolina and go to a strange state. I remember I even took a cut in pay (from $11,000 to $9,000). I was so enthralled being able to coach basketball full-time at a university."

From Kentucky she took a coaching job at Oral Roberts University in Tulsa, OK, where she met her future husband, Dr. William Bowden. "I had a student athlete who was not doing well in one course, and someone recommended talking with Bill. He was a

My parents were shocked that I would leave North Carolina and go to a strange state. I remember I even took a cut in pay.

Don't let anyone tell you that you're not feminine if you play a sport. You can do anything you want to do. Women need to experience team sports; it's important to understand being a team player in today's workplace.

professor in education and also an administrator who often counseled students. I remember we shook hands as fellow professionals and said 'Nice to meet you.' He paused, then said 'You're kinda cute for a coach.' I thought that was very unorthodox! He began coming to the women's games, and we started dating."

Debbie and Bill married and, in 1983, took jobs at the University of Florida in Gainesville. Debbie coached the Lady

Gators basketball team, getting their first national ranking in the AP Top-Twenty. Two years later she was offered a new administration position, raising money for the University of Florida Gator Boosters, the most successful fund raising group in the country at that time. She was the first woman hired to raise money (all the staff were men). "Bill and I made a family decision that I would retire from coaching earlier than planned, because we believed an opportunity like this might not come along again."

Debbie found that the skills and techniques she used as a coach, especially in recruiting new athletes, helped her ask for donations. Within 3 months she brought in her first gift, $50,000 from three women who had supported her as a coach and together wanted to sponsor a special basketball scholarship for women. "Bill Carr, Florida's athletic director, was a wonderful mentor, as was John James. Their advice guided me as I learned fund raising and athletic administration."

From this position, Debbie moved to Associate Athletic Director for External Affairs and Director of The Spartan Excellence Fund at the University of North Carolina in Greensboro. Three years later she became Director of Athletics at Saint Louis University. Her excellent success at Saint Louis paved the way for her move in 1994 to the University of Maryland.

While Bill has his own work as a nationally known accreditation consultant, he also works with Debbie as a volunteer, helping out especially in any writing she does. "Right now there are only seven other women athletic directors. When we attend an athletic directors' conferences, he is the 'spouse' and spends his time with all the wives. He enjoys it. He's always taken pride in me and my work. His support is very important to me."

HEAD ATHLETIC TRAINER

Lisa White

HEAD ATHLETIC TRAINER, **Adelphi University**, Garden City, NY
HEAD ATHLETIC TRAINER, **New York Liberty**, Women's National
Basketball Association

Major in Liberal Arts; master's degree in Sports Management

Athletic Trainer

PLAYERS' PAINKILLER

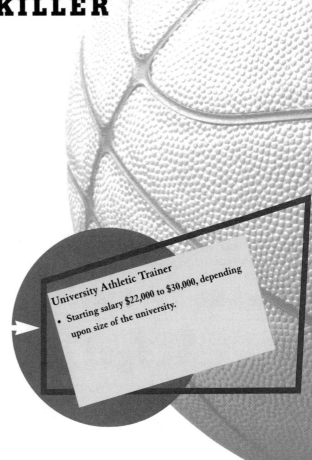

As the basketball game starts, Lisa White carefully watches the players she knows so well. She worked recently to prevent knee injuries and checks to see if they learned the correct moves. Before the game, she taped the wrists and ankles of some athletes. She makes sure they're doing okay. She is alert, because if a player is injured, she will be one of the first people out on the court to help.

As athletic trainer Lisa works directly with the players. She is responsible for the care and the prevention of injuries. She helps individuals stay in good physical condition and works with them to overcome any weaknesses that may develop. She helps athletes prevent injuries, teaching them what their bodies can and cannot do and how to protect themselves.

University Athletic Trainer
- Starting salary $22,000 to $30,000, depending upon size of the university.

Starts playing basketball at age 5

Plays basketball in college, discovers athletic training

Gets graduate assistant position earns masters

When injuries occur, Lisa determines what is wrong and what needs to be done for healing. When injuries are minor, like

player gets to the team's doctor, and she consults with the doctor in setting up the rehabilitation program. As head athletic

> **You can learn so much from being on a team—discipline, how to work hard, how to budget your time. You get a lot more out of it than the wins and losses.**

a sprain, Lisa treats them and sets up the exercises the player must do to rehabilitate. If injuries are severe, she sees that the

trainer, Lisa makes the decision as to when the injured player is well and able to play again.

Teaches at Adelphi
▼ Physical Education
Department

Promoted to head
▼ athletic trainer

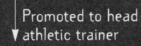

Works summers for
▼ New York Fever

"There's a lot of pressure from the coach to get the athlete right back in the game. You have to build that relationship so the coach will trust your decisions. I'm not there to keep athletes from playing, but to make sure when they go back they're not going to further injure that body part. It is my decision."

"The athlete is also eager to play. We explain what the injury is. We have body-part models to show what was injured and what we're doing to heal it. When they understand, it makes it easier for them."

At the university, Lisa has a full-time assistant and a graduate assistant to help her run the training room operation for the school's 16 sports. In the mornings, she usually takes care of paperwork like insurance. Rehabilitation appointments take place from 11 a.m. to 2 p.m. Then athletic trainers help the players get ready for practice or a game—doing stretches, getting taped. The games take place late afternoon or evening and on weekends, and Lisa or one of her assistants is at every

LISA'S CAREER PATH

Joins N.Y. Liberty as head trainer/business manager

Inducted into school's Hall of Fame

practice and every game. (They also travel with the team.) Afterward, the players go back to the training room for any treatments they need, like icing or cleanup of minor scrapes.

Lisa works 6, sometimes 7 days a week,

especially during the Fall when athletes play lacrosse, soccer, and volleyball. She also teaches classes in basic and advanced athletic training, and she supervises student trainers.

"Every day is different, and I like not having a set schedule. I love working with athletes. If I can help them perform, teach them techniques to avoid injury and to strengthen muscles, it's very rewarding. And if there's injury, I enjoy helping them regain their performance. It's great." Lisa concentrates on two areas—lifting weights and stretching—where athletes often use incorrect techniques. "A big part of conditioning is using right techniques. For example, in weights, it's not how much weight you lift, but whether you do it correctly. We also teach correct throwing and tackling."

New York Liberty

During the summer, when the university athletes are not on campus, Lisa has fewer responsibilities. So, Adelphi supports her role as the athletic trainer for the New York Liberty, a Women's National Basketball Association (WNBA) team whose season runs from mid-May through August.

When Lisa heard that the WNBA was forming and that New York would have a team, she sent a letter with her resume There were 5 athletic trainers interviewed, but Lisa got to help the team in this part-time job. She is responsible for attending Liberty's daily practices and games. She sets up conditioning and strength-training programs for individual team members and supervises their rehabilitation when needed. She is also the team's business manager, and she arranges the team's travel—getting tickets, arranging meals and places to stay, and keeping track of travel expenses.

In the Fall of 1997, Lisa traveled with

CAREER CHECKLIST ✓

You'll like this job if you ...

- Can relate to athletes' experiences, understand them

- Are an outgoing person, positive, with a sense of humor

- Are flexible, don't get upset if plans change

- Will work long hours

- Easy-going, enjoy working with people

- Can listen to people complain, like to help them

GROUNDBREAKERS

Helen Stevens, from a small town in Missouri, set a world record and won two gold medals in track and field at the 1936 Olympics. She went on to become the first woman owner/manager of a women's semi-professional ball team and a lifetime sports advocate.

WNBA's European Tour. The chosen 12 players from 8 teams had games with Germany's national team and a professional team in Italy. "I was chosen to go because they took the head coach and assistant from New York. After the two games we did some sight seeing in Paris. The players visited high schools and hospitals. It was interesting to meet the European players. Their definition of professional is to play 3 times a week, and many of the players have other jobs. Our teams play or practice every day. We won both games."

Basketball's Dynamic Duo

Lisa is an identical twin. She and her twin sister, Michele, were born and raised in Richmond Hill near New York City. Lisa still lives in the same house, downstairs. Her mother and younger sister live upstairs. Her two older brothers have their own homes, and Michele, a physician's assistant in orthopedics, recently moved to Florida.

The coach I played for
was very tough.
He'd yell and scream, but
I thought he was great.
When he was there
he gave us 150 percent, and
that's what he
demanded from us.
It's not always a
bad thing to have someone
who is demanding
your best.

"Michelle and I did everything together. We started playing basketball, our favorite sport, when we were 5 years old. We played basketball and softball in high school. We decided we wanted to continue playing in college and chose the State University of New York at Stony Brook." The twins roomed together and made the team together. Michelle, who is the school's all-time leading scorer for basketball (women's and men's), was inducted into the school's Hall of Fame in 1997. Lisa was inducted in 1998.

"I never knew what an athletic trainer was until Michelle got injured during our sophmore year," says Lisa. "The athletic trainer evaluated her injury, pinpointed what was wrong, and set out the steps she had to follow to get back her performance, pain free. That's what really introduced me to the work. At Stoney Brook, there was no physical education degree, but you could take the courses needed to become an athletic trainer and get a liberal arts degree. The National Athletic Trainers' Association lists the courses you have to take—like anatomy, physiology, kinesiology, psychology, and nutrition. After you earn your degree, you must pass the 3-part exam (written, oral, and simulation) to get certified."

Lisa started on her master's degree at Hofstra University, Hempstead, NY, where she got a position as a graduate assistant. Then she got a graduate assistant position at Adelphi University and stayed on after she earned her master's degree in Sports Management. "The graduate assistant position is really the way to go. You're working in your field, but getting your schooling paid for."

In Her Spare Time

Lisa's love of basketball and sports shows up in her leisure activities and work outside of Adelphi. For vacations, she likes outdoor activities like a sailing trip or bike riding.

During the winter, she plays in a women's basketball league once a week. "I really look forward to it. I get to see a lot of the women I went to college with." She is a New York State Girls Basketball Official and referees high school basketball.

During summers before she joined the Liberty, Lisa provided daily instruction and supervision at a basketball camp in Southampton, NY. It was started by her coach from Stony Brook. One summer, she worked with the Olympic Development Program Youth Soccer Camp. She also traveled with the group's international tours for 3 years. "On Long Island, soccer is big. Every April they sent two teams, about 30 girls, to Europe. The teams played about six games each in two cities. There was sightseeing too. We were gone about 9 days."

In 1994, Lisa was contacted by a professional men's soccer team, New York Fever. "It was great. I worked with them for two summers. The level of play was very professional." But she had to give it up when she began working for WNBA's New York Liberty during the summer.

Even though she is now working two jobs and has little time off, Lisa is enthusiastic about her work with Liberty. "It's new and exciting. It's professional, it's women's basketball, and I just enjoy being around it."

SPORTS PSYCHOLOGIST AND PROFESSOR

Colleen M. Hacker

SPORTS PSYCHOLOGIST AND PROFESSOR, Pacific Lutheran University, Tacoma, WA

SPORT PSYCHOLOGIST, U.S. Women's National Soccer Team

Major in Health and Physical Education; master's in Exercise and Sports Science; Ph.D., Exercise and Movement Science

Sports
Psychologist

SHE TAPS THE POWER OF THE MIND AND HEART

There has never been a time when Dr. Colleen Hacker didn't love her work. Maybe that's the secret to her astonishing career. A coach, professor, assistant dean, writer, researcher, and sport psychologist, Colleen is a super achiever who is always pushing for her own personal best. She spends her time divided between her three great loves—teaching in Pacific Lutheran University's School of Physical Education, sport psychologist for the U.S. Women's National Soccer Team, and consultant and lecturer for universities and sport associations.

Colleen has spent the past 19 years at Tacoma, Washington's Pacific Lutheran in teaching and coaching positions. Pacific Lutheran is a small school with a rel-

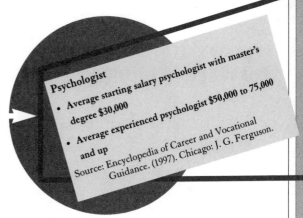

Psychologist
- Average starting salary psychologist with master's degree $30,000
- Average experienced psychologist $50,000 to 75,000 and up

Source: Encyclopedia of Career and Vocational Guidance. (1997). Chicago: J. G. Ferguson.

Plays field hockey, basketball, and badminton in high school

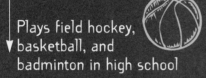

Plays three sports in college, graduates with 3.9 GPA

Goes to Olympic trials in team handball and field hockey

atively small athletics budget. Under Colleen's coaching, the university women's soccer team played for the NAIA (National Association of Intercollegiate Athletics) national championship in 5 consecutive years and won NAIA titles in 3 of them. Colleen's winning teams make her first among all coaches in NAIA women's soccer history. When Pacific Lutheran won its first national championship in 1988, it was the first time a woman head coach had led a collegiate soccer program to a national title.

Believe in the possibilities of your own greatness and be prepared to do the work that is necessary. I believe everybody has the capacity to do great things.

Earns master's degree, coaches and teaches at University of Arizona

Accepts job as coach and professor at Pacific Lutheran University

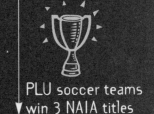

PLU soccer teams win 3 NAIA titles

Ignored Advice

Pacific Lutheran was an unlikely place for Colleen to end up. A star athlete from the time she was a small girl, Colleen always took the unconventional path. "The people I've most respected and are closest to professionally have always advised me to do other than what I did," she says. "After getting my master's degree, I had all kinds of offers to coach at Division I universities. After getting my Ph.D., I was told I needed to be at a major research institution. Everybody had an opinion about what I should do, but none included my passions. I had grown up in an era when all the best teachers were coaches and all the best coaches were teachers. What I most valued was to be a college faculty member and a university coach at the same time. That's the job I took. I'm not an either/or gal."

As a teacher, coach, and sport psychologist, Colleen has had a rich and varied career. "I have standards that make me throw myself into everything I do with the same energy. I know what something requires, and I doggedly pursue it and nothing stands in my way. When there is a problem, I just find a way to solve it. I wanted to do things in an environment

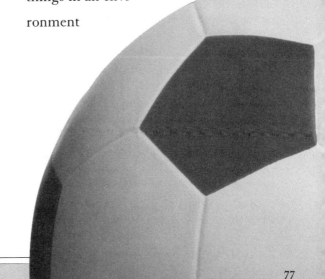

COLLEEN'S CAREER PATH

Gets Ph.D.

Becomes sport psychologist
for U.S. Women's National
Soccer team and they win
1996 Gold Medal -

and in a way that is true to who I am and what I'm about. The teaching and coaching have kept me at the University. The job changes every year. When I came here, our soccer team was much more like every other team in America than it was different. But the difference was our heart and our beliefs, our collective spirit. I truly believe in bringing out the best in yourself and then bringing out the best in others. It's not something I say; it's something I live."

When Colleen isn't teaching, giving lectures at other universities, or serving on sport association com-

mittees, she is the official sport psychologist for the U.S. Women's National Soccer Team, and the national girls' and young women's soccer teams that feed that team. In this position, she interacts with the top girl and women athletes in any age group playing soccer in the United States. She was the sport psychologist for the 1996 U.S. Olympic Women's Soccer Team. They won the gold medal, the first given to a U.S. team in Olympic women's soccer.

Training the Brain and the Heart

It was in her junior year in college when Colleen took a course in the psychology of coaching; something clicked with her. "It really fit my interest in sports, which was primarily emotional," she says. "I have never found anything as emotionally compelling as sports. What it's like to achieve and accomplish, what it's like to fall short— these things fascinate me. It's so interesting to see normally reasonable, calm, rational people get into a sport and become totally different. A whole new world opens up for them. And sport psychology has allowed me to study sport systematically and at a scholarly level. I love how sports illustrate that things people think are out of their control really aren't. Why do some people thrive in adverse circumstances? In the same way, you can make a muscle bigger by training it, sport psychology allows you to make your brain and your heart bigger by understanding the power that you have inside you."

During a typical day with the U.S. Women's National Soccer team, Colleen will go to all the practice and training sessions the athletes attend so she can see and understand the training regimen. Then there are several individual sessions each day with members of the team who want

CAREER CHECKLIST

This career is for you if you ...

- Believe in yourself and others

- Are passionate about sports

- Never give up on anything

- Like to help people do their best

GROUNDBREAKERS

Wilma Rudolph is the first

American woman ever to win three

gold medals in the Olympics.

A track and field champion,

she gave women's track a major

presence in the United States.

She created the

Wilma Rudolph foundation to

help train young athletes.

to improve specific areas of their play. Colleen acts as the soccer player's "mental coach." There are also presentations to the entire team about communication, trust, problem solving, and leadership. The days are long, beginning at 7:30 a.m. and ending 9:00 p.m. or later.

"When I'm working with the National Soccer Team, there is no time for reading or preparing," she says. But on days when she is back at the university, she spends a good part of her time reading sports and physical education journals to keep up with the latest developments in the fields of sport psychology and physical education. At the university, she teaches sport psychology to physical education majors.

Competitor at 5

How did a girl from a small farm town in rural Lancaster, Pennsylvania, end up as a world-class coach and sport psychologist to some of the best athletes in the world? Colleen's parents encouraged her in sports activities at the age of five, when she was involved in competitive swimming. Along the way, she had some strong women coaches as role models who inspired her. Her swim team was one of the top summer swim teams in the state. She took horse back riding lessons throughout elementary school. She played field hockey and basketball in junior high and high school until she broke her ankle and added badminton. Then she got herself ranked second in East Coast singles and mixed doubles in tournament badminton. "Anything and everything related to sports, I was doing it," she says, "round the clock, 12 months a year."

Colleen also was a top student. "My parents had to tell me to quit studying so hard, rather than urging me to study." She held the second highest GPA in her high school and graduated with honors from college with a 3.9 grade point average.

On Her Own at 15

But Colleen had her share of hardships as a teenager. When she was 15, her parents moved to Australia to join her brother, who was a champion surfer there and had been a big influence in Colleen's life. But she decided she wanted to stay in the United States. Left without close family, she rented the third floor of local family's house, worked as a groom for race horses in the morning, took a full load of classes in school, played sports, and then worked in a shoe factory at night. "Most people think I led a charmed life, but that couldn't be further from the truth," she says. "I had my share of adversity. I think that's why I got hooked by sport psychology. It was about overcoming limitations."

Even before her first year in college, Colleen knew she wanted to teach at the university level and to do research. She did her undergraduate work at Lock Haven University in Pennsylvania, a school she chose because she had played for the basketball coach during a summer basketball camp and knew she wanted to continue playing for her. During her college years she was invited to the first Olympic trials for team handball. She was in the Olympic trials for field hockey the

her master's program, a school ranked in the top 10 in exercise and sport science. The school attracted her because she would have the opportunity to study with Donna Mae Miller, a pioneer in coaching female athletes, and Dr. Jean Williams,

I had my share of adversity. I think that's why I got hooked by sport psychology. It was about overcoming limitations.

same year. It's very unusual to try out for two Olympic sports in the same year, but Colleen was such a good athlete and so versatile that she was encouraged to do it.

She chose the University of Arizona for

an internationally renowned sport psychologist. Colleen's first coaching job was there as an assistant coach for field hockey at a Division I school. While she was studying for her master's, Colleen also taught activity classes at Arizona. This showed her she could do coaching, teaching, and studying simultaneously. Later, when she studied for her Ph.D. in exercise and movement science at the University of Oregon, she also was teaching and coaching, this time at Pacific Lutheran. The school gave her a leave of absence so she could pursue her doctoral work at Oregon. "I look back and it seems impossible that I was able to do that, but at the time, I didn't analyze it, I just did it. It was what I wanted to do."

BASKETBALL OFFICIAL

Renee Paugh

BASKETBALL OFFICIAL, Ellicott City, MD

Major in Business Administration—Management

Basketball Official

SHE CALLS THE SHOTS

Renee Paugh arrives at the NCAA Division I, women's intercollegiate basketball game an hour and a half before game time, as requested. She checks in with the game management. She gets into her uniform, then meets with the other two officials who make up the crew that is working the game. "We have a pre-game conference to discuss how we're going to cover the floor and situations that may happen." Arriving on the floor, the officials meet the table personnel who will keep the official record of the game statistics.

The conference supervisor, who hires the officials for the conference games, assigns the officials to their position for this game. One is the head referee, the others umpire one and umpire two. While all

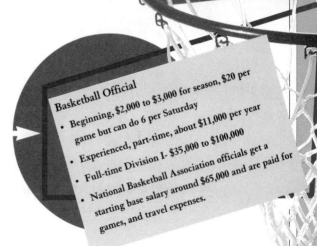

Basketball Official
- Beginning, $2,000 to $3,000 for season, $20 per game but can do 6 per Saturday
- Experienced, part-time, about $11,000 per year
- Full-time Division I- $35,000 to $100,000
- National Basketball Association officials get a starting base salary around $65,000 and are paid for games, and travel expenses.

Played sports in
neighborhood

Excelled at high
school sports

Basketball
scholarship to
college

It takes time to work your way up, but if you give 150 percent, people will recognize that. It's also good exercise, a great way to keep fit.

three will call fouls, no official has the authority to set aside or question decisions made by the others within the limits of their respective outlined duties.

Renee covers her area of the court. "Basketball is a game of angles. We have to be in the best position on the court to see things. That's what our pre-game conference is about. From one angle I could see a foul, but it could look clean from another angle. We want to keep the players boxed in and have an angle from all sides."

"There is a saying, don't anticipate the

Married Dan

worked at NSA, played
basketball, golf, tennis

Had two children

call, anticipate the play." Renee knows what a player is likely to do because she played basketball in high school and college. She is comfortable making split-second decisions, blowing her whistle to stop the clock.

The game is over in a couple hours, and Renee heads for home. Whenever she can, she arranges to get home that night, so she'll be there in the morning to get her 7-year-old son, Branden, ready for school and to take care of Megan, 5 years old.

This is Renee's ninth year as a basketball official. She has multiple contracts with NCAA Division I, II, and III conferences, plus junior college, all along the East Coast. Renee officiates about 80 games per year, which are held from November to February, then come the postseason tournaments. She travels by car to most games, but has flown as far as Boston and Tallahassee. For Division I and some Division II games, Renee receives a game fee, plus travel and a per diem (a set amount of money that covers meals and lodging if appropriate). For the other games, she receives only a game fee.

"You have to keep track of your assign-

Work as part-time official   Signed Div I contracts

ments, so paperwork is important. And you keep track of expenses, because you are an independent contractor, in business for yourself. You keep your supervisors informed. You want them to know your open dates in case they need you to substitute. I keep a calendar and like to have the week ahead all planned. I'm not a last-minute person. I want to be sure I have a good baby sitter lined up."

ball team. That year they only played 5 games because few schools had a girls' team. But the next year, 1976, more schools had teams. In high school, Renee played basketball, volleyball, golf and made all state in all three sports.

When Renee graduated in 1980, women's basketball wasn't very big, but there were scholarships. She was recruited by Auburn, Maryland, Old Do-

Always played sports

Renee grew up in Huntington, WV. A natural athlete, she enjoyed playing all kinds of sports. She played basketball mostly with neighborhood boys until seventh grade, when she played on the school's basket-

minion—Old Dominion's team was national champion at that time. But she was super shy then and decided to accept a full scholarship at a small church school, Freed Hardeman College, Henderson, TN. It was a Division III school. "I thought, what am I going to do with basketball after college? There was no women's professional team. I knew in a Division I school all my time would be taken with one sport. In the Division III school I was able to play two intercollegiate sports—basketball and tennis."

Renee's major was Business Administration with an emphasis in management.

CAREER CHECKLIST ✔

You'll like this job if you ...

↑

Love the game of basketball

Can make quick decisions

Are organized and can manage your time

Will keep healthy and fit

Like to travel

Respect people involved in sports

↓

GROUNDBREAKERS

Billie Jean King dominated the world of tennis for more than 20 years. She won 20 Wimbledon titles and 13 U.S. Open titles. She founded the Women's Tennis Association and helped create the Women's Sports Foundation.

She wanted to graduate in 4 years and took a full course load. But because of her sports and the required Bible classes that don't count toward a degree, Renee went to summer school at Marshall University in Huntington to get all her credits. She met her future husband there. "We dated long distance because Dan went to West Virginia University. He is a year older. When he graduated, he got a job with the U.S. Department of Defense and moved to Maryland. The next May, I graduated, and we married in June."

Renee applied for a job at the National Security Agency (NSA), where Dan worked. She worked in marketing jobs until she got her security clearance from NSA and a job as a contract specialist. During this time, Renee played basketball with a recreation league and Dan became a basketball official. "The referee board that Dan belonged to would referee my games. He and his friends were after me for 3 years to become a referee. They needed women officials. But I was super shy, and I don't like conflict. I did not want people yelling at me in my spare time."

Training Starts at the Kids' Games

Renee finally was persuaded to take a class and began training in October, 1989. Then she discovered she was pregnant. "So my first year of refereeing 80 ball games I was pregnant. But I didn't put on much weight, so I didn't show. And I enjoyed it."

Renee got over her shyness. As to avoiding conflict, she found that at her first games the kids were fine. It was the parents who were the problem. "But most of the parents didn't really know the rules, so the criticism didn't really apply. But now, if a coach says something about a call, I will take a look at it. I could be missing something."

Beginning officials get some on-court training before doing a game, then they start with kids' games. "There are observers from your supervisory board that rate you and give you feedback. You have to 'pay your dues' and work your way up from kids games to junior varsity, then high school, Division III, Division II, and Division I. It is very competitive."

In the summer, officials go to camps—learning or tryout camps. At learning camps, beginners referee high school games, often with someone at their shoulder, moving up and down the court with them. Costs for the intensive 4- to 5-day camps range from $200 to $300.

Experienced officials go to tryout camps to get 'picked up' by college conference supervisors, much like top athletes are chosen. Cost range from $300 - $450. "There are no guarantees. Just because you had a contract the year before, you may not get renewed. You need to attend the camps to show that you want to improve, work on your skills, and learn any changes in the rules."

When the supervisors are selecting officials at the camps and when they observe them during the playing season, they are looking for special qualities, says Renee. "There are a lot of good officials. What separates them is what the supervisors call game management. How do I handle a coach who is on my case? How do I control myself? How do I interact

You don't get into this for the money, but because you love the game. The game was good to me and this is a way I can give something back to the game!

with the players, with the other officials, with the table personnel? How is my appearance, my confidence, and my fitness?"

A Promising Future

Women's professional basketball just got organized in 1996 with the American Basketball League (ABL) and in 1997 with the Women's National Basketball Association (WNBA). Two women officials were hired by the men's National Basketball Association (NBA) in 1998. The opportunities for women officials are increasing.

"In our area, high school students are encouraged to train as officials. I have helped train them at kids' games. If someone is at all interested, they could start to get experience in high school.

Then they could do it through college for extra income. When they graduate with that experience, they could possibly pursue college basketball."

Renee's future calls for more of the same. "I'm happy where I am now. I'm busy from November through March, and I'm off in the summers except for the camps I attend. My husband is very supportive. My goal is to get more Division I games, but be here for my family also, because of the way I feel about my kids. I really enjoy it."

EXECUTIVE DIRECTOR

Jackie Shannon

EXECUTIVE DIRECTOR, Women's Soccer Foundation
ATHLETIC DIRECTOR, New Testament Christian School, Norton, MA

Major in Elementary Education

Foundation Director
High School Coach

SOCCER'S PRIZE COACH AND BOOSTER

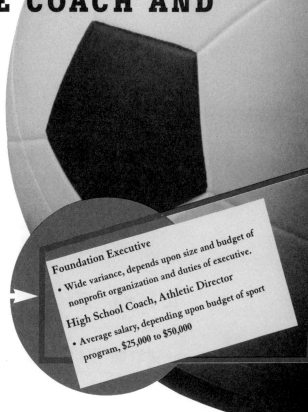

A s executive director of the Women's Soccer Foundation, Jackie Shannon promotes girls' and women's soccer internationally. In her other job as athletic director at a private high school, she is responsible for its athletic programs. She is one of only a few women athletic directors in Massachusetts' high schools. "Athletics is still very much male-dominated," she says. "But positions for women are beginning to open up."

As the Foundation director, Jackie helps arrange soccer meetings and training clinics geared toward girls and women in cities throughout the United States. She helps publish a quarterly newsletter about girls' and women's soccer around the world. It is her responsibility to get sponsors for what she calls

Foundation Executive
- Wide variance, depends upon size and budget of nonprofit organization and duties of executive.

High School Coach, Athletic Director
- Average salary, depending upon budget of sport program, $25,000 to $50,000

JACKIE'S CAREER PATH

Plays basketball
in gym after her
custodial work

Graduates
college with
Elementary Education

Works in softwa
marketing

soccer symposiums, which combine training sessions with lectures from experts. She also has to find contributors whose money will help to promote

and she's often on the telephone. She thinks she is really lucky to be able to work from home so much. That means she can spend more time with her

When I was young, if you didn't play with the guys, you just didn't play.

women's soccer internationally. And she lines up speakers, coaches, and locations for the Foundation's events, which help to keep everyone excited about the Third Women's World Cup Soccer games scheduled the summer of 1999, the first to be held in the United States.

Jackie works at home much of the time,

2-year-old son, Cody. Jackie's husband, Jim, has his own business and can watch Cody when needed because his schedule is flexible.

Before Cody was born, Jackie spent her days at New Testament Christian School (NTCS) teaching various subjects, coaching soccer, and running the school's athletic and fund-raising programs. During her second year, NTCS hired her to also be the athletic director. When she started at NTCS, the athletic programs were weak. "I changed the school colors from maroon and gray to red, white, and black (more exciting), enrolled the school in a league (which helped them get more publicity in the newspapers), and established a real budget for sports, not just the occasional car wash, "she says. "I didn't get as much resistance as I thought I would in trying to build up the sports program. It wasn't long before the student and parents began to take more pride in their school athletic program. Today we have boys and girls' soccer, basketball, softball and baseball—all varsity level— and next year we are thinking about starting a golf team. It's very rewarding to see what we've accomplished. The students are quite excited about our programs."

When her son was born, Jackie retired from teaching, but continued to coach and serve as athletic director, and she would do a good part of her work from home. She spends part of most days on the telephone, scheduling games, organizing fields, finding officials to referee, getting the newspaper to publicize the events, and checking to make sure that every detail is in place for the games. "After you've done this for a number of years, you pretty much know what needs to be done and you just do it," she says.

Jackie didn't want to give up coaching completely after Cody's birth, so she still coaches a soccer team in the fall. "I love soccer. But then I love whatever sport I'm involved in. I still play basketball and love that too." In the summer, she is a director and coach at a soccer camp called Soccer Future. "Today, I can pretty much pick and choose those activities and events that are most important and appealing to me. When I first started working, I worked longer hours to do everything."

Teaching the Coaches

On winter weekends, Jackie teaches novice youth coaches how to coach soccer. The courses are geared to provide technical and tactical information, and to give the coaches confidence, which will help make their teams more successful. "There are different levels of soccer coaches. They go from the most novice—Gs—to As. You have to be certified at the national level to be an A coach, but once you have that certification, you can coach just about anywhere."

In 1995, Jackie coached kids who were trying out for the regional feeder pools for the Olympic Development Program. Although coaching these elite athletes was enjoyable, Jackie's first love is coaching her high school team. "It's always interesting to see what talents the fresh crops of kids have, coming in. We have baseball and basketball athletes who just play soccer for fun, but they have the best time during soccer season. We've made the state tournament in 4 out of 6 years.

As the smallest school in the state, that's quite an accomplishment."

As a girl, Jackie loved sports. She played catch, softball, and football in the back yard with her dad. She had two brothers, but neither of them were as interested in sports as she was. "I always played with the guys," Jackie says. "When I was young, if you didn't play with the guys, you just didn't play." She played everything in junior high. And, although she longed to play athletics in high school, circumstances didn't allow it. Instead she got a job as a school custodian so she could save money for college. "The best thing about the job was that we had the gym to ourselves after we finished our work. A bunch of us would spend hours playing basketball."

Jackie saved enough money to pay for nearly all her college education. The rest she covered with a small loan. She grew up in New Hampshire, but she went far away to college, to Pensacola Christian College in Florida. Even though she wanted to major in physical education so she could be a player or a coach, her dad convinced her to study things that would

You'll like this job if you ...

Are flexible, patient, and persistent

Are very organized

Can pay attention to lots of details

Are tactful and have a good sense of humor

When you're operating in a man's world, you sometimes will get sexist remarks thrown at you. There are two ways to deal with this.

give her a better chance of getting a teaching position when she graduated. "This was really good advice," she says. "I often hear students and parents talking about college athletic scholarships. Most kids have no idea how competitive college sports are. Only 2 percent of all college students get athletic scholarships, and the chances are very slim to even play on a Division I college team. Girls who are interested in a sport should continue to play it as much as possible, but think about their education before the sport. It really worked for me. It got me this great job, where I can coach as much as I want."

It's Not the Money

Jackie's first job out of school was not in sports. It was with Digital Equipment Corporation in their software marketing department. "I had worked for them when I was in college and they hired me full-time after grad-

You can either
disarm them with humor but
let them know they've
overstepped the boundaries,
or you can be more direct.
I usually choose the
humor route.
The other way, you run
the danger of cutting off
contact with those people
you really need to
interact with.

GROUNDBREAKERS

Clara Baer, who taught physical education for 38 years at Sophie Newcomb College, introduced to New Orleans both the game of basketball and the first rules for women in 1895.

SOURCE: What Women Have Done calendar, Library of Congress.

uation. At first it was great—my own office (well, cubicle) and the alluring world of high tech. But then I found myself going to meetings when the weather was beautiful and I wanted to be outside coaching. After a year I decided to get into teaching and coaching. It was a big step. I remember, I had just gotten to the point where I was making decent money. One day I was driving my manager somewhere, and when she got out she had trouble closing the door of my old car. 'I hope you know what you're doing,' she said. 'Teachers don't make much money.' But I know I made the right choice. I love what I do. I haven't looked back."

About the same time she left Digital, Jackie met her future husband. It was an Easter dinner at a family friend's house. The Red Sox game was on TV, and she mentioned she loved the Red Sox. This sparked a conversation with her future husband. It was love at first sight. Shortly after this, Jackie applied for an internship to Park School in Brookline, MA, just outside Boston. She got both teaching and coaching experience there, and that opened the door to her current career.

Her first full-time teaching position, though, was a disappointment. It was at a small school in another Massachusetts town. She wilted when she saw how little attention the school paid to sports. After a year she looked for another position and found NTCS. Even though New Testament didn't have the best athletic program, they seemed to be willing to build the program up, which her first school didn't want to do.

"I wrote down my goals in college. They were to live in Massachusetts, be involved in coaching, and work with my husband. I'm doing all of these," says Jackie, who often helps Jim with his golf marathon business. "It's a great life. I wouldn't trade it for anything."

PRESIDENT AND CO-FOUNDER

Ellen K. Wessel

PRESIDENT AND CO-FOUNDER, **Moving Comfort**, Chantilly, VA
Major in Sociology

Entrepreneur

A FIT AND POWERFUL WOMAN

In 1974, when Ellen Wessel started jogging and running, the only appropriate clothes available were designed for men, and women wore them.

"It didn't immediately occur to us that the fit problems we had with the clothes had to do with who they were being made for," says Ellen. "We 'knew' for sure that if we were skinnier, the clothes would work. When the light finally went on, we realized that it wasn't our bodies that were at fault—the clothes were made for skinny men. With the coming together of three key elements, our business was born in March 1997. One, we pretty much hated our jobs. Two, we loved running. Three, no one else was bothering to make running clothes for women."

Ellen and her partner Valerie Nye

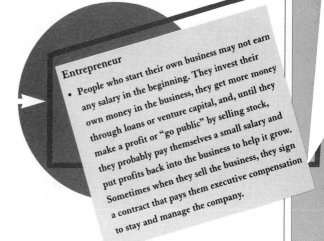

Entrepreneur
- People who start their own business may not earn any salary in the beginning. They invest their own money in the business, they get more money through loans or venture capital, and, until they make a profit or "go public" by selling stock, they probably pay themselves a small salary and put profits back into the business to help it grow. Sometimes when they sell the business, they sign a contract that pays them executive compensation to stay and manage the company.

made a down payment of $75 on a Singer sewing machine and began taking orders from their runner friends. The first thing

a square. After writing an article for the then-new *Running Times* magazine and getting an ad for payment, they got letters

I am the investigative reporter, getting answers, finding out what we need to know, finding the sewers, the shippers, the sales people.

they did was change the shape of the running shorts from a rectangle to more like

from retail people asking for a catalog. So their next effort was to produce a catalog.

As orders began coming in, their direction was decided—they would sell the clothes through specialty retailers like Human Race, Marathon Sports, Track Shack, REI, and Foot Works.

By Fall, the business was growing, but not providing a living. Valerie, who had a husband and young son and had to work, could not continue. Ellen, who was single, had savings, and a small inheritance from her father (who died when she was 8 years old). She quit her job as a congressional liaison at the U.S. Department of Housing and Urban Development (HUD). She moved the business into the bedroom of her one-bedroom apartment. Through friends, she met her new partner, Elizabeth Goeke. Elizabeth was working as an apprentice tailor at a department store. By March 1978,

Elizabeth quit her job and joined Moving Comfort as a full partner. "We cut and sewed and tried the clothes on, and ran in them, hiked in them, washed the car and emptied the trash in them, and critiqued, altered, and adjusted." In 1982, Ellen's cousin Andy Novins became the third partner, bringing finance and operational skills.

From that small beginning, Moving Comfort grew, and then survived some lean times in the mid 1980s (when many

competitive companies like NIKE began to supply runners' clothes). Today it is a profitable business with $12 million in sales. "Our product category is performance athletic wear for women and suitable for layering. The sport underwear for support and comfort that wicks away perspiration, the shorts and tops for comfortable fit, and jackets and long pants for warmth, and wind and water protection."

A balanced schedule

Ellen has, at one time, worked most of the jobs that her staff now hold. These include areas such as product development, manufacturing, shipping, sales, and accounting. Today, her time is spent on communicating with people, developing visibility for the Moving Comfort brand name, working with special projects such as the catalog, and managing resources to make sure that staff have what they need to succeed at their work.

Believing in having a balanced life, she takes time off from the business for the outdoor activities that she loves—horseback competitions, biking, hiking, and running. She owns her own home, has two (indoor) cats, and has created a bird habitat in her 20' x 22' back yard.

Ellen starts her day at 7 with a run, then showers, grabs a banana, and drives 6 miles to the office. While her days are not routine, she usually starts by checking her voice mail and email messages. She writes memos, makes phone calls, and sees what is scheduled for the day. Perhaps she checks the shipping forecasts, or attends a meeting with the design group working

You'll like this job if you ...

Believe in your idea with a passion

Are able to convince and persuade others

Are resourceful and tenacious

Are a good problem solver

on a brochure, or meets with the sales representatives about an upcoming trade show. Her current project is to reevaluate how the company is organized and staffed, and there are informal meetings with staff and partners. Ellen and Elizabeth often lunch together in the office.

Ellen is actively involved with industry and consumer organizations and serves on the boards of SGMA (Sporting Goods Manufacturers Association) and Outdoor Recreation Coalition of America. She keeps in touch by phone and travels to attend board meetings. She also travels to do public speaking and to meet with suppliers. She calls these mini-vacations. For learned to better understand each other's styles of communicating to avoid misunderstandings and arguments. "Communication is so important in everything we

In high school, I was so wrapped up in boy friends and superficial things. I feel I wasted a lot of time.

example, she is planning a trip to visit one of the plants in Costa Rica that sews Moving Comfort's clothes. "After the meetings, we partners have planned a hike into the mountains."

The partners Ellen, Elizabeth, and Andy each have different talents and skills. With the help of business psychologist Dr. Bob Rosen of Healthy Co., they do. The complement of skills we have among ourselves is essential to the success of the business."

Ellen attributes her success to her passion, tenacity, persistence, and resourcefulness. "I am the investigative reporter, getting answers, finding out what we need to know, finding the sewers, the shippers, the sales people. Elizabeth is the designer, creating the products. Andy is skilled in the financial and operations areas. I focus on problem solving."

At the end of a regular day, if it's Tuesday or Thursday, Ellen heads home, changes to her riding clothes, and drives a few miles to where her two horses are stabled. "My idea of a vacation is to stay home and ride every day."

Active Outdoor Life

Ellen grew up New Rochelle, NY, with an older and younger brother and played outdoors a lot. "We rode bikes, rollerskated, sledded, rode horses, and played in the woods. In those pre-Title IX times, I never considered sports. In high school, I thought being a secretary would be a good job for me. I was so wrapped up in boy friends and superficial things. I feel I wasted a lot of time."

Ellen graduated from the State University of New York at Binghamton with a degree in Sociology. She moved to Washington, DC, where her older brother lived and got her first full-time job with a newspaper. She next worked as publications director at the Kennedy Center for Bioethics, then quit to become a volunteer for the Carter Campaign in 1976. Following Jimmy Carter's election as President of the United States, she took a job as a congressional liaison at HUD.

When Ellen took up running, it became a passion. She joined groups, raced in local events, and within 2 years was entering marathons. Ellen told her family about her decision to start her own business, and they were very supportive. Her mother even helped set up her first bookkeeping ledger.

"I have a high sense of integrity, I was brought up that way. If you are honest and represent yourself accurately, you will be effective. When we promised a catalog, we went to work and delivered a catalog. I believe when you make a commitment, you follow through to keep it. We're still keeping that commitment."

"A fit woman is a powerful woman" is not only the company's slogan, but also expresses its mission, which is to encourage girls and women to get fit and stay fit to improve every aspect of their lives.

Ellen started running for fitness as her second try to quit smoking, which was making her ill. "For thousands of women like me, running was the perfect route to developing physical strength and testing endurance, because success is based more on character than it is on coordination." Now, a retired marathoner (nine), she only occasionally runs in events.

"Since our beginning we have supported, and we will continue to support, women athletes and women-centered sports events in order to foster fitness among girls and women of all ages."

I have a high sense of integrity, I was brought up that way. If you are honest and represent yourself accurately, you will be effective.

WHAT TO DO NOW

To help you prepare for a career in sports, the women interviewed for this book recommend things you can do while in middle school, junior high, and high school:

Lisa White, athletic trainer.
Team Sports: Prepare and go to college, even if you don't know what you want to do. Participate in team sports. So many doors open once you're there, you'll find something interesting you are able to pursue.

Julieta Stack, golf professional.
Golf: If you think you have any shot at tour play, if that is what interests you, play every amateur event you can get in. Play every chance you get in high school and college, then go for the qualifying school. Get a sponsor. Work harder than anyone else. Always have a good coach you trust, because golf is a lonely game. Your coach knows you and your swing, but bottom line is hard work. Don't think it will come easy. Prepare for the struggle. When you are successful, it's worth it.

Mary Beth Quinn, ski and snowboard instructor.
Skiing: If you're really interested in teaching skiing and snowboarding, find a resort where you can learn to teach as a junior instructor while you're still in high school. Then, when you are in college, you have a great part-time seasonal job compatible with school schedules. During that time you can train to earn PSIA certification (Professional Ski Instructors of America), which will allow you to find a job as an instructor at any number of ski areas in the United States.
It's good to get a recreation management degree if you want a career in the ski industry. That way you will be able to market more than one skill to all kinds of resorts. You could become a recreation director or be involved in sales and marketing. All ski resorts are now four-season re-

sorts, offering a multitude of activities and services to their guests. This allows a position's job description to change with the season, adding variety to one's career.

Robin Roberts, sports broadcaster.
Sport Journalism: If you're thinking about sports journalism, read widely and take as many different courses as you can. Acquire an impressive command of the English language.

Tammy Jackson, professional basketball player
Basketball: Get your grades so you'll be able to get to college and play. It's also important to have an idea and prepare for what you want to do when your athletic career is over.

Renee Paugh, basketball official.
Official: If you are at all interested in officiating, start to get experience in high school. Then you can do it through college for extra income.

Ellen Wessel, entrepreneur.
Entrepreneur: Start a business. My partner Elizabeth made bags and sold them in high school. Get a strong liberal arts education. Learn to communicate in writing and public speaking. In business you are always interacting with people. Develop a work ethic, take responsibility, make promises and keep them. Get to know yourself. Envision what kind of day you want to be living and what is important to you. Then make it happen.

RECOMMENDED READING

A Whole New Ball Game: The Story of the All American Girls Baseball League by Sue Macy. (1993).
Winning Ways by Sue Macy. (1996). NY: Henry Holt and Co.
The Stronger Women Get, The More Men Love Football by Mariah Burton Nelson. (1994). Orlando: Harcourt Brace & Co.
Are We Winning Yet? by Mariah Burton Nelson. (1991). NY: Random House.
Encyclopedia of Women in Sports in America by Carol Oglesby. Phoenix: ORYX Press.
Coming on Strong by Susan Cahn. (1994). NY: Macmillan.

For women's sport history try:

National Women's History Project

7738 Bell Rd., Windsor, CA 95492-8518

(707) 838-6000

email nwhp@aol.com

Most every sport has one or more magazines devoted to it. Magazines like *Sports Illustrated* and *Sports Illustrated for Kids* cover many sports.

References:

Encyclopedia of Career and Vocational Guidance. (1997). Chicago: J. G. Ferguson

Career Opportunities in the Sports Industry by Shelly Field. (1991).

Peterson's Scholarships, Grants, and Prizes. (1997). Princeton, NJ: Peterson's.

http://www.petersons.com

PROFESSIONAL GROUPS

Check these groups for information, clinics and conferences, programs for juniors, and certification guidelines. Many sports not listed here have organizations. Check in your library for the *Encyclopedia of Associations*, published by Gale Research.

General

National Association for Girls and Women in Sports, (also has a Division called National Coaches Council that recruits, develops, promotes women for coach positions.)

1900 Association Dr., Reston, VA 20191

(703) 476-3450

email nagws@aahperd.org

This is part of the larger American Alliance for Health, Physical Education, Recreation and Dance, same address, phone (703) 476-3400, which also includes National Association for Sport and Education, phone (703) 476-3410.

Women's Sports Foundation

Dedicated to increasing opportunities for girls and women in sports and fitness through education, advocacy, recognition and grants.

> Eisenhower Park
> East Meadow, NY 11554
> Infoline (800) 227-3988, voice (516) 542-4700, fax (516) 542-4716
> email wosport@aol.com
> http://www.lifetimetv.com/WoSport

National Collegiate Athletic Association (NCAA)

> 6201 College Blvd., Overland Park, KS 66211
> (913) 339-1906
> http://www.ncaa.org

National Association of Intercollegiate Athletes (NAIA)

> 6120 S. Yale, Ste. 1450, Tulsa, OK 74136
> (918) 494-8828

Athletic Trainers

American Sports Medicine Association and Board of Certification

Grants the CSMT (certified sports medicine trainer)
> 660 West Duarte Rd., Arcadia, CA 91007
> (818) 445-1978

American Athletic Trainers Association

> 146 E. Duarte Rd., Arcadia, CA 91006

Basketball

American Basketball League

> 1900 Embarcadero Rd., Ste 110, Palo Alto, CA 94303
> email hoops@ableague.com
> http://www.abl.com

Women's National Basketball Association

> 645 Fifth Ave., New York, NY 10022
> (2121) 688-9622
> http://www.wnba.com

Women's Basketball Coaches Association

4646 Laurenceville Way., NW, Ste B; Lilburn, GA 30247-3620

(770) 279-8027

Golf

American Junior Golf Association (ages 13-18)

2415 Steeplechase Lane, Roswell, GA 30076

(770) 998-4653

Ladies Professional Golf Association

100 International Dr., Daytona Beach, FL 32124-1092

(904) 274-6200

Professional Golfers Association of America

100 Avenue of Champions, Palm Beach Gardens, FL 33418

(407) 624-8400

Officials

National Association of Sports Officials

2017 Lathrop Ave., Racine, WI 53405

(414) 632-5448

Affiliated Boards of Officials

1227 Lake Plaza Dr., Colorado Springs, CO 80906

(719) 576-7777

Skiing and Snowboarding

Professional Ski Instructors of America

Certification program for instructors

133 Vinegarden, Lakewood, CO 80228

(303) 447-0842

National Collegiate Ski Association

P.O. Box 100, Park City, UT 84060

(801) 649-9090

Soccer

Women's Soccer Foundation

> P.O. Box 2097, Norton, MA 02766
>
> (508) 285-5699
>
> http://www.womensoccer.org
>
> United States Soccer Federation
>
> certifies coaches
>
> 1801-1811 S. Prairie Ave., Chicago, IL 60616
>
> (312) 808-1300

Sport Psychologist

American Psychological Association

> Videos available on careers in psychology
>
> 750 First St., NE, Washington, DC 20002-4242
>
> (202) 336-5707

Sport Journalism

National Sportscasters and Sportswriters Association

> Box 559, Salisbury, NC 28144
>
> Association for Women in Sports Media
>
> P.O. Box 4205, Mililani, HI 90789
>
> (808) 525-8040

Tennis

U. S. Professional Tennis Association

> One USPTA Center
>
> 3535 Briarpark Dr., Houston, TX 77042
>
> (703) 978-7782

Many sports organizations and sports magazines have sites on the Internet. Check out Just Sports for Women at http://www.justwomen.com.

How COOL Are You?!

Cool girls like to DO things, not just sit around like couch potatoes. There are many things you can get involved in now to benefit your future. Some cool girls even know what careers they want (or think they want).

Not sure what you want to do? That's fine, too... the Cool Careers series can help you explore lots of careers with a number of great, easy to use tools! Learn where to go and to whom you should talk about different careers, as well as books to read and videos to see. Then, you're on the road to cool girl success!

Written especially for girls, this new series tells what it's like today for women in all types of jobs with special emphasis on nontraditional careers for women. The upbeat and informative pages provide answers to questions you want answered, such as:

✔ **What jobs do women find meaningful?**
✔ **What do women succeed at today?**
✔ **How did they prepare for these jobs?**
✔ **How did they find their job?**
✔ **What are their lives like?**
✔ **How do I find out more about this type of work?**

Each book profiles ten women who love their work. These women had dreams, but didn't always know what they wanted to be when they grew up. Zoologist Claudia Luke knew she wanted to work outdoors and that she was interested in animals, but she didn't even know what a zoologist was, much less what they did and how you got to be one. Elizabeth Gruben was going to be a lawyer until she discovered the world of Silicon Valley computers and started her own multimedia company. Mary Beth Quin grew up in Stowe, Vermont, where she skied competitively and taught skiing. Now she runs a ski school at a Virginia ski resort. These three women's stories appear with others in a new series of career books for young readers.

The Cool Careers for Girls series encourages career exploration and broadens girls' career horizons. It shows girls what it takes to succeed, by providing easy-to-read information about careers that young girls may not have considered because they didn't know about them. They learn from women who are in today's workplace—women who know what it takes today to get the job.

personality checklist for each job

sts of books to read and videos to see

alary information

upportive organizations to contact for scholarships,

mentoring, or apprenticeship and intern programs

✔ What skills are needed to succeed in each career
✔ The physical demands of the different jobs
✔ What the women earn
✔ How to judge whether you have the personality traits to succeed in the different jobs
✔ How much leisure time you'll have
✔ How women balance work and relationships
✔ Reasons for changing jobs
✔ The support received by women to pursue their goals
✔ How women handle pregnancy and child care
✔ What you need to study to get these jobs and others

ORDER FORM

Title	Paper	Cloth	Quantity
...ool Careers for Girls in Computers	$12.95	$19.95	_____
...ool Careers for Girls in Sports	$12.95	$19.95	_____
...ool Careers for Girls with Animals	$12.95	$19.95	_____
...ool Careers for Girls in Health (June 1999)	$12.95	$19.95	_____
...ool Careers for Girls in Engineering (July 1999)	$12.95	$19.95	_____
...ool Careers for Girls with Food (August 1999)	$12.95	$19.95	_____
		SUBTOTAL	_____

A Residents add 4½ % sales tax _____

...ipping/handling $5.00+ $5.00

.50 for each additional book order (__ x $1.50) _____

TOTAL ENCLOSED _____

...HIP TO: (street address only for UPS or RPS delivery)

...ame: _____

...dress: _____

I enclose check/money order for $_____ made payable to Impact Publications

Charge $ _____ to: ☐ Visa ☐ MasterCard ☐ AmEx ☐ Discover

...rd #: _____ Expiration: _____

...gnature: _____ Phone number: _____